Beginners Basic Guide to Investing in Gold and Silver Boxed Set

This boxed set includes:

- **Investing in Gold and Silver Bullion - The Ultimate Safe Haven Investments**

- **Economic Crisis: Surviving Global Currency Collapse - Safeguard Your Financial Future with Silver and Gold**

Beginners Basic Guide
to Investing in Gold and Silver Boxed Set

I thank God for His exceeding grace.

Beginners Basic Guide to Investing in Gold and Silver Boxed Set

Beginners Basic Guide to Investing in Gold and Silver Boxed Set

By

Alex Uwajeh

Beginners Basic Guide to Investing in Gold and Silver Boxed Set

Legal Disclaimers

All contents copyright © 2012 to and written by **Alex Uwajeh**. All rights reserved. No part of this document or accompanying files may be reproduced or transmitted in any form, electronic or otherwise, by any means without the prior written permission of the publisher.

This book is presented to you for informational purposes only and is not a substitution for any professional advice. The contents herein are based on the views and opinions of the author and all associated contributors.

While every effort has been made by the author and all associated contributors to present accurate and up to date information within this document, it

Beginners Basic Guide
to Investing in Gold and Silver Boxed Set

is apparent technologies rapidly change. Therefore, the author and all associated contributors reserve the right to update the contents and information provided herein as these changes progress. The author and/or all associated contributors take no responsibility for any errors or omissions if such discrepancies exist within this document.

The author and all other contributors accept no responsibility for any consequential actions taken, whether monetary, legal, or otherwise, by any and all readers of the materials provided.

It is the readers sole responsibility to seek professional advice before taking any action on their part.

Readers results will vary based on their skill level and individual perception of the contents herein, and thus no guarantees, monetarily or otherwise, can be made accurately. Therefore, no guarantees are made.

Beginners Basic Guide to Investing in Gold and Silver Boxed Set

Investing in Gold and Silver Bullion - The Ultimate Safe Haven Investments

Introduction: Why Gold and Silver?

There are two large categories of metals: precious metals and base metals. This categorization is based on the metal's ability to resist oxidation and corrosion. Precious metals have a higher resistance to corrosion while base metals have a much lower tolerance.

In this book, we will be looking at two precious metals: gold and silver. We will look at the fundamentals of these precious metals and show you *why* and *when* it's a good idea for your investment portfolio to have some exposure to these precious metals. From what drives their price, including how they can be used as a gauge of investor sentiment regarding the stability and future of the economy, to investment vehicles, this guide will help you gain a better understanding of gold and silver.

All that Glitters May Not Be Gold...

...but its value cannot be denied. For thousands of years, gold has been used as a form of currency and has not lost its inherent value. Its metallurgical properties have made it a highly valued asset throughout the centuries, including its virtual indestructibility and rarity.

The Properties of Gold

Gold is one of the few metals to have an incredibly high level of resistance to corrosion. Exposure to oxygen, for example, has practically no effect on this metal, allowing it to retain its properties for thousands of years with no change.

In terms of rarity, you are likely well aware that this is one of the rarest resources on the planet and in over 6,000 years, ever since gold was first mined, only about 150,000 tons of gold have been extracted in total. This is a tiny amount, especially when compared to other metals.

Another advantage gold has is that it is a very malleable metal, making it easy to shape into almost anything.

This has made gold one of the favourite metals for jewellery makers all over the world. However, it is often mixed in alloys with other metals to allow it to retain its shape because in pure form (24K), it can be too soft to wear.

Ductility is a measurement that refers to how much wire a certain amount of metal can produce. For example, one ounce of gold can be converted into more than 50 miles of wire that can be used in a variety of electronic applications, making it incredibly valuable in this industry.

The Value of Gold to Investors

Gold's properties have allowed it to maintain its value for thousands of years, which makes it a great investment vehicle. However, you will find there are two schools of thought when it comes to gold and other precious metals. There are those who believe gold is a great hedge against currency devaluation and feel investing in gold is a wise course of action at any time, especially for capital preservation.

Then, on the opposite end of the spectrum are those who believe gold is a waste of time and money because it no longer has any value in the digital age and will soon be worthless to everyone.

While there will always be naysayers, no one can deny the fact that gold's value has remained unchanged since recorded history, which is why it was even used as currency for a lot longer than we have had paper money and fiat currencies. In fact, even when we switched to paper money, gold was still used to back the currency and it was only in 1971 that the gold standard was eliminated by President Nixon. Many feel this decision was what led to the continued devaluation of the dollar.

But wait, the price of gold fluctuates thousands of times daily. How can anyone say its value has remained the same? It's a good question and the answer is quite simple. We all try to determine the value of something based on price, i.e. its dollar value. However, the dollar, or any currency, is just a piece of paper so a true measurement of value would be how much oil you can buy with an ounce of gold. Or, how much food you can buy, for example.

24 Hour Gold Price Chart spanning 5 days courtesy of www.GoldSilver.com

Two or three centuries ago, you could buy a high quality suit or clothes with an ounce of gold and the same holds true today. So, gold hasn't actually changed its value. It's the currency that has appreciated or depreciated over time, which is one of the factors driving the price of gold. We'll take a closer look at precious metal prices a little later.

Besides the stability of gold's value, there are other considerations that make it an attractive investment, including some of the industries it is used in. There is a high demand for gold in the jewellery sector, as you probably imagined, but it is also a highly coveted metal in the electronics industry, as well as in dentistry. The more industries use a metal, the higher the demand for that metal will be, which will often drive prices up even further.

Is It Time to Melt the Silverware?

Jewellery and silverware represent a small percentage of the silver market, as this metal has wide range of practical applications, from technology to healthcare and photography. In fact, over 65 percent of total silver consumption can be attributed to the industrial sector. Due to the fact that it has a high resistance to corrosion and oxidation and because of its numerous practical applications, silver has always been considered an attractive investment.

Silver Applications and Demand

Silver is used in a wide range of sectors, from fashion to décor, technology and industry. However, you might not realize exactly how widespread the use of silver is. For example, in recent years, the technology sector has expanded its use of silver massively.

It is one of the best thermal and electrical conductors in the world, which, in combination with other properties it has, makes it the only suitable option for certain applications. Not only is it used in electrical components but it is also used as a coating material for data storage media, such as DVDs. Essentially, almost all the electronic devices we use today have some degree of silver in them.

Additionally, it is also used in the photography sector, in water purification, and even in windows and glass. There are so many applications for this precious metal that demand has soared over the past ten years and currently the supply of silver cannot meet the demand.

Beginners Basic Guide
to Investing in Gold and Silver Boxed Set

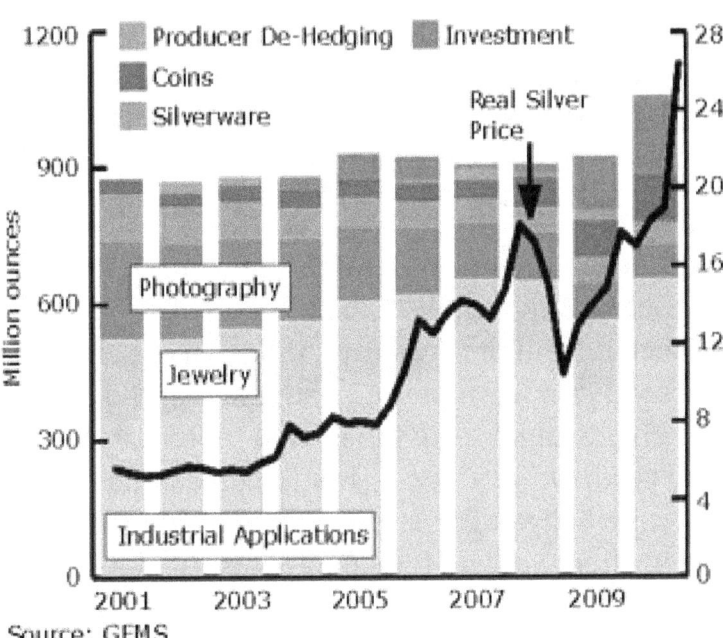

This increase in demand is one of the factors that has influenced the price of silver, driving it up significantly, as you can see in the previous chart.

The Value of Silver to Investors

Similar to gold, silver has long been considered a safe investment, especially to hedge against inflation. Like gold, silver is a precious metal and has been used historically as a currency. While not quite as rare as gold or some other precious metals, it is still relatively rare and its unique properties have allowed it to maintain its value over many thousands of years.

It is considered to be a low-risk and cost-effective investment, especially since it is relatively protected from the volatility of the financial markets. It is worth noting, though, that the cost or perceived value of silver is much more volatile than gold. Despite this, it is still considered an effective hedge against currency devaluation and an excellent vehicle for capital preservation.

Many investors opt for silver because it offers a level of stability due to its intrinsic value. Including silver in their investment portfolios is also another step they can take to diversify their assets, thus protecting their wealth against market volatility.

Currencies, the Gold Standard and Precious Metals

The gold standard was in use in the US until 1971. This meant the value of the US dollar was pegged to the value of gold. However, as European and Asian countries began buying up US gold reserves, President Nixon decided to eliminate the gold standard and the dollar, as well as any other currency that followed suit, has been declining in value ever since.

The devaluation occurred mainly because governments had no other option than to create additional currency to combat short-term economic crisis, as the recent financial meltdown is testament to.

Other economic policies were adopted that further damaged the value of currency, including extending cheap credit, which resulted in spending by both organizations and individuals that could not be supported for the long-term, tax breaks, interest rate changes to support cheap lending, and foreign borrowing, which increased the deficit.

However, an interesting process began to occur: as the value of the dollar against gold dropped.

The value of precious metals began to rise. This is because investors began to see these commodities as the only safe haven in an economy where the value of currency had begun to plummet. As the chart below shows, gold was selling for approximately $40 per ounce in 1971, a price it had been hovering around for more than two decades, only to double in less than two years. A decade later it was selling for a massive $615 per ounce, an increase of 1,500%

Evolution of the Price of Gold
1970 - 2011

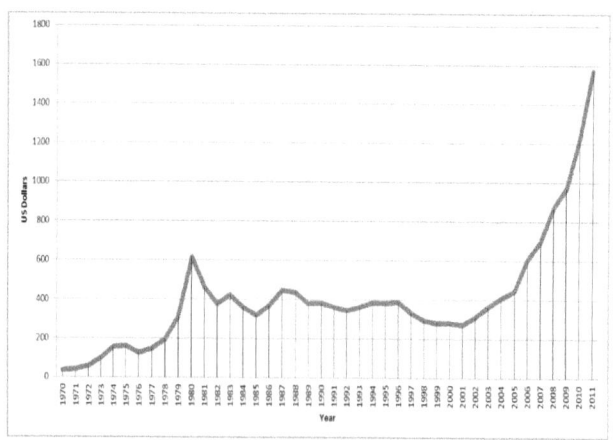

Beginners Basic Guide to Investing in Gold and Silver Boxed Set

So, how does the elimination of the gold standard affect the current market?

Due to the financial meltdown of 2008 and the fact that many economies have not yet recovered, with many countries still hovering on the verge of recession, countries are continuing to create more currency to try and prop up their economies. Of course, the term used nowadays is quite elevated: quantitative easing.

Quantitative easing simply means the central banks have decided to pump new currency into the market, in the hopes of stimulating the economy. However, while more cash might stimulate spending, it simply means injecting more paper money into circulation. This leads to further devaluation of the currency in question, which is why we are seeing price increases across the board.

As the dollar loses value, many investors are turning to precious metals, converting at least part of their investment portfolio from cash, equities and other assets into silver and gold in an attempt to preserve the value of their capital. This is why the price of gold has more than doubled since 2007, when it was selling for approximately $695 per ounce. In 2011, the average price of one ounce of gold was $1,571.

Three Reasons to Invest in Precious Metals

So, why should you invest in precious metals, especially gold and silver?

Capital Preservation

Capital preservation is probably the most common objective of investors when they invest in precious metals. Essentially, they are hedging against currency devaluation. It is a way for them to protect their wealth.

Think of it as the equivalent of purchasing insurance on your home. If your house catches fire, you will receive the full value of your property from your insurance policy. The same applies to purchasing gold and silver.

As we've already discussed, even if the currency drops in value, gold and silver will maintain their value, which makes them an ideal investment vehicle for anyone looking to preserve their capital. However, remember that if you are purchasing gold and silver with capital preservation in mind that means you are basically expecting the dollar to drop in value.

Capital Appreciation

Just because precious metals are a safe haven and often used as a hedge, it doesn't mean they can't be used for capital appreciation as well.

Through speculation, you can buy and sell precious metals and make a profit, especially in an economy such as this one, where the prices of gold and silver have been rising steadily over the past few years.

However, you have to remember that the only way you will really make a profit is if the devaluation of the dollar is slower. Otherwise, you will be simply preserving your capital and in this situation it's probably smarter to hang on to your gold and silver.

Cash Flow

Another reason to invest in gold and silver is for cash flow purposes. In other words, you're aiming to create an additional income stream. Basically, it's like purchasing a property that you intend to rent out. It will bring you an annual income for as long as you own it, irrespective of its value.

There are many benefits to this approach. First of all, you will be hedging your wealth by owning gold and silver, but you will also be making profit every year.

Essentially, it doesn't really matter how the value of these precious metals fluctuates because you will still be making money every year, so you can afford to hang on to these assets for the long term and won't have to worry about the volatility of the markets.

There are a few ways you can use gold and silver to generate cash flow. The first is through short-term speculation, i.e. commodity trading. Essentially, you purchase gold or silver and sell it within a relatively short timeframe for a profit. This could be anywhere from a few minutes to a few months, depending on your trading strategy.

Another method is to invest in these precious metals via dividend stocks in mining companies. The advantage to this approach is that you can grow your wealth by reinvesting your dividends into more equity. However, remember that via this approach you won't actually be holding physical gold and there are other factors affecting the price of shares, including the company's fundamentals, which are often unrelated to the price of gold. We'll look at more investment vehicles for precious metals later on.

The State of the Economy and Precious Metals

The state of the economy can often be used as a gauge for the price of precious metals. The worse the economy is performing, the more the price of precious metals will rise. One way to determine where the economy will be heading is to look at the GDP and deficit.

The GDP or Gross Domestic Product is basically everything a country produces and sells, which is what brings money to the state via taxes. If the GDP is low relative to the deficit, then the only solution for most governments is to print more currency. This leads to further currency devaluation.

For example, the US is predicted to be approximately $16.5 trillion in deficit by November, 2012. However, that's not the only problem. The baby boomers are soon going to hit retirement age and the social security and healthcare systems will have to deliver, meaning the government has massive off-balance-sheet promises to keep to these people alone. So, it could be a while before the situation improves.

Another gauge of the economy, and a way to really determine how dire the situation is, is by looking at the price of credit-default swaps. When a country has a high level of debt and a low GDP, sentiment regarding its ability to pay off its debt on time is far from positive. So, to ensure that debt credit default swaps are purchased, CDS indexes are used by traders to determine the credit quality of a country or company. This is because the more the price rises, the worse the situation is.

Therefore, if you see the price of credit default swaps soaring, then the market might be telling you it's a perfect opportunity to purchase precious metals.

Currently, for example, the price of European CDSs is at an all-time high, meaning the situation isn't looking good and printing even more currency seems to be the only solution. This will lead to further devaluation and investors will turn to precious metals as a hedge, driving the price up even further.

And the future certainly doesn't look bright, with Europe hovering on the verge of recession, even with the austerity measures that have been instituted. There is even talk of some countries leaving the Eurozone and returning to their original currencies. This will only lead to massive inflation within those countries as they print more and more of their own currencies to try and cover the deficit.

Even the US doesn't look quite as rosy as some believe, with the deficit continually on the rise. In fact, it's very likely spending will continue to increase, which will probably lead to further need for quantitative easing and it is likely we will see the value of the dollar fall even further as a result.

What Influences the Price of Gold and Silver?

There are many factors that influence the price of precious metals but these are some of the most important ones.

Market Sentiment

All markets are driven by trader and investment sentiment to a certain degree.

If you've ever traded, you will know how various pieces of news affect the markets, with price becoming highly volatile during release of said news. And this is not just in regards to economic news. The political situation in a country, for example, or even just rumoured social unrest can frighten traders and that country's currency can plummet in value as people lose faith and market sentiment turns negative.

In fact, quite often market sentiment drives prices on the markets more than any other factor, simply because it is the reaction of traders to economic news and reports that leads to the buying and selling of assets, which drives supply and demand on the markets.

For example, in terms of equities, even if a company posts good results, its stock prices can fall if a rumour is started. If a rumour is started claiming the company is considering cutting dividends, let's say, to increase the proportion of the profits it is allocating to growth and reinvestment. It could be a simple rumour and hold no truth at all, but if the source is 'credible' then value investors will rush to offload their stocks before the price drops too far. Gold and silver react in much the same way. In the late 1990s and all the way up to 2007, investors avoided gold like the plague. It was a time of massive economic growth and everyone was looking towards asset classes that would bring massive profits. No one wanted to hear about gold because it doesn't offer interest, nor is it traditionally a profitable investment. It was, and still is, mainly used for capital preservation, and at a time of massive growth in other asset classes, no one was interested in capital preservation. Everyone was running after capital gains, especially since the market was offering massive returns.

Let's not forget all the derivatives that appeared on the market as financial institutions found new and better ways to make money by inventing more and more complex financial instruments most investors had a hard time understanding. However, market sentiment was along the lines of "why understand it when I can make a fortune off it?"

When traders were posting massive returns from trading everything from equities to currency, who wanted gold? There was no need for capital preservation. The economy was booming and there was no end in sight. That was until 2008, when the bubble burst in a highly spectacular way.

Suddenly, gold was the safe haven every investor was clamoring to buy, especially after they had been burned so badly when the stock market took a plunge that forced some from riches to rags.

As a result, the price of gold climbed from approximately $695 in 2007 to over $1,600, which it is trading at now, at the beginning of 2012.

Currency

The value of gold is quoted in US dollars but it is mainly purchased by individuals using other currencies, which means the price of gold will go up as the dollar drops. There are two ways to look at it. First, if viewed as a commodity, the falling dollar would mean negative investor sentiment, leading to increased buying of gold.

On the other hand, if gold is considered a currency, then when the dollar falls, gold has to rise by definition and the reverse is also true.

It is important to note that while there is some correlation between the dollar and the price of gold, the gold market doesn't move in the same way as other precious metal markets. For example, when it comes to silver, the main driver is supply and demand. The higher the demand and the lower the supply, the higher the price will climb. However, when it comes to gold, things are a little different.

The price of gold tends to show more restrained movement in response to decreased supply and production. One reason is because there are large stockpiles of gold, which can't be said for silver. Thus, if central banks feel the price of gold is too high, they can release some of their reserves to drive the price down. So, essentially, the market tends to place less weight on news related to supply and demand when making its trading decisions.

The currency component is one of the main factors affecting the price of gold in the long term, and even silver to a certain degree. As currency devalues, more and more investors turn to precious metals as a hedge, driving up the price of these precious metals.

Interest Rates

An environment of low interest rates is positive for almost any asset class, including precious metals. However, for precious metals, high interest rates made them a commodity everyone wanted to avoid. Why invest in an asset that couldn't possibly deliver.

Well, this situation lasted for a while, until it was decided the economy needed further stimulation and interest rates began to drop, allowing cheap credit to be extended to the population.

The results of that decision, as well as highly lenient banking regulations and other policies, are rather obvious.

Mining

Another factor influencing the price of precious metals, especially gold, is mining.

The fact is that production has decreased significantly over the past few years, because there is little gold available in 'easy-to-access' conditions.

Essentially, all the 'low-hanging fruit' has been mined and any new discoveries are usually in areas that are very difficult to mine. You can see how production cost are rising when you consider the fact that it can take a decade to get all the permits required to mine this precious metals. One shouldn't forget that there are other factors influencing production costs, including the rising prices of other resources required to mine gold.

Portfolio Diversification and Precious Metals

After the recent financial crisis, an ever increasing number of financial institutions, including private banks, pension funds and hedge funds have turned to the commodity markets to diversify their portfolios.

The more currency is printed, the more gold and silver they purchase because they know gold will always maintain its intrinsic value and many of these organizations are currently looking more to preserve their capital than necessarily making profit.

This is mainly due to the fact that physical gold is highly liquid, making it easy to sell in any market conditions. Even in the worst case scenario, where currencies become worthless, physical gold can still be traded for goods because of its intrinsic value.

And these large market movers are not the only ones turning to gold and silver as a hedge. More and more retail investors are allocating part of their portfolio to gold and silver in an effort to preserve their capital.

How to Get Exposure to Gold and Silver

There are a wide range of methods for the individual investor to gain exposure to precious metals. Whether you are interested in physically owning gold and silver in the form of coins or bullion, or prefer to go for less traditional options such as mining stocks and other more complex financial instruments related to precious metals, the best precious metal investments will largely depend on how you view the future and what your personal goals are.

Even if you do want to invest in physical gold or silver, don't worry because there are plenty of options available to you without you having to take physical delivery.

Physical Gold: Bars and Coins

The first gold coins were struck by King Croesus during his reign in western Asia Minor. Ever since then, gold coins have been considered a form of legal tender.

The advantage for the retail investor when it comes to coins and small bars is that you don't have to buy massive quantities to be able to include gold in your investment portfolio. The fact that gold purchased for investment purposes is exempt from Value Added Tax in many countries is an added bonus.

Gold Bullion Coins

There are plenty of options when it comes to gold bullion coins because many governments across the world issue this form of tender. In the countries they are issued, the value is not based on the content of gold but rather their face value.

Conversely, when it comes to global market value, it is calculated based on the fine gold content with a premium added, which differs depending on the coin and dealer.

The smaller the coin, the higher the premium will be as it covers production costs as well as the dealer's commission.

Coins come in a variety of sizes, starting from as small as $1/20^{th}$ of an ounce all the way up to 1,000 grams. However, the most widespread sizes are 1/20, 1/10, 1/4, 1/2 and one troy ounce of fine gold content. Remember that bullion coins have nothing to do with commemorative or numismatic coins. These are valued according to the quality of their design and finish as well as their rarity and not their fine gold content like bullion coins.

Below are some examples of gold bullion coins minted by different countries.

South African Krugerrand

Australian Kangaroo

Beginners Basic Guide
to Investing in Gold and Silver Boxed Set

American

American

Britannia

Images courtesy of Gold Bars Worldwide

Gold Bars

There are two types of gold bars, depending on how they are manufactured. Thus, there are cast and minted bars. Gold bars themselves are considered to be any gold item, irrespective of its shape, that was produced by a recognized bar manufacturer. They are usually sold at a price that consists of the value of the fine gold content plus a low premium. Usually, the markings featured on the bars tend to reveal the name of the manufacturer, the weight of the bar and the level of gold purity. Some bars also feature a serial number. The characteristics of bars tend to change according to the manufacturer and the area they are produced. Furthermore, gold bars are categorized by weight. Thus, small gold bars are considered to be equal or below 1,000 g (approximately 32 oz), while large bars are those weighing more than one kilogram.

Small bars are generally preferred by investors due to the lower entry barrier and smaller investment of capital required at one time. There are more than 50 different weights of small bars worldwide, providing investors with a wide range of options.

Gold purity generally is around 99.5% but it can vary slightly between manufacturers. If you wish to further investigate accredited bar manufacturers and the international gold bar market, please visit the Gold Bars Worldwide website at www.goldbarsworldwide.com.

Gold Futures and Options

Another option for investors looking to get exposure to gold is via gold futures and options.

Gold Futures

Like any other futures contract, gold futures represent a binding commitment to deliver or accept delivery of a certain quantity of gold at certain level of purity on a pre-determined date at a pre-agreed price. Investors pay a cash deposit to the broker, referred to as the initial margin, and represents only a small percentage of the underlying asset.

The advantage to gold futures is that you can make significant trading profits because you can buy a lot more gold than if you were to purchase it in physical form. However, it should be remembered that they can also lead to significant losses. Futures contracts are traded on regulated commodity exchanges, with the largest being the New York Mercantile Exchange Comex Division, now known as CME Globex, the Chicago Board of Trade and the Tokyo Commodity Exchange. These futures also trade on the India and Dubai commodity exchanges.

Gold Options

Gold options give their owner the right to buy (call options) or sell (put options) a certain amount of gold at a pre-agreed price and on a set date. Note that it is merely the right and the owner is not obligated in any way to fulfill the contract.

The price of options depends on a wide range of factors, including interest rates, volatility, time until they expire, the spot price of gold and the pre-agreed price.

Beginners Basic Guide to Investing in Gold and Silver Boxed Set

Metals: Open Interest (in thousands)

Open Interest 12/27/2011			Change from Last	
			Month	Year
Gold	Futures	418.9	-4.2	-175.5
	Futures & Options	624.2	-22.6	-179.2
Silver	Futures	104.0	5.0	-33.9
	Futures & Options	138.6	6.6	-45.9

Chart courtesy of the Commodity Futures Trading Commission

Gold Exchange Traded Funds

Exchange Traded Funds (ETFs) backed by gold are traded on many stock exchanges all over the world.

These are financial instruments that are regulated and meant to offer investors the opportunity to gain exposure to gold price.

ETFs are a great way for investors to integrate gold into their investment portfolios because they are cost effective and highly secure. Additionally, it is also more efficient because you don't have to take actual delivery of the gold. ETFs are responsible for the increase in attractiveness of gold as a way to diversify one's investment portfolio.

Gold Warrants

Similar to futures and options but mainly used by leading investment banks, gold warrants give the holder the right to purchase gold at a specified price at a particular future date. As with futures and options, the buyer pays a premium for this right, allowing them to lock in a certain price and make a profit if the market moves in the forecasted direction.

Gold Accounts

Bullion banks, which are those banks that deal in precious metals, offer investors two types of gold accounts. Thus, there are allocated accounts and unallocated accounts.

Allocated Gold Accounts

The allocated gold account is similar to keeping your gold in a safe and is considered to be the safest way to invest in physical gold because the gold is held in a special vault that a dealer or repository owns and manages. Bars or coins are created and stamped with a number and hallmark. They are then allocated to the individual investors who also pay a premium for insurance and storage, besides the standard price of the bullion they are purchasing.

Note that if you choose this route, you own the gold and are simply using the dealer's services so you don't need to worry about issues such as storage. This means the holder of the gold, i.e. the dealer, may not lend, sell, borrow, lease or do anything with those gold bars unless it is at your specific instructions.

Unallocated Gold Accounts

There is one problem, namely that bullion banks tend to deal only in large quantities so if you are intending to open an account with less than 1,000 ounces, you might have to look at other options. This is because they generally work with institutional customers such as private banks, central banks and large participants in the gold market.

Gold Pool Accounts

These are a good option for the smaller investor who wants to open an account with less than 1,000 ounces. Basically, you are buying a share in a Gold Pool Account and can purchase as little as one ounce.

Electronic Currencies

Another option is the electronic currency. There are some electronic currencies available that are backed by gold bullion which is in an allocated account. This is a simple and inexpensive way to buy and sell gold, with the advantage of being able to use it as money as well. You can purchase any quantity of gold you like and you can use it to make payments online all over the world.

Gold Accumulation Plans

Gold Accumulation Plans or GAPs are like a traditional savings plan except instead of setting cash aside every month, you convert it into gold. So, say you get paid on the 30th of every month and you want to allocate $500 every month to your GAP. That money would then be deducted from your paycheck and used to purchase gold on the first trading day after the cash hits the account.

The advantage is that you can allocate small amounts of cash every month and you won't have to pay the premium coins and bars usually come with.

Additionally, since you are buying small amounts of gold regularly, over a long period of time, you will not be as exposed to short-term volatility in gold price.

The contract is usually for a minimum of one year but afterwards you can terminate it and either pick up your gold in the form of coins or bars. You also have the option to sell the gold and get cash instead.

Gold Mining Stocks

A popular option, especially for investors looking for capital gains, is purchasing equity in gold mining companies. This offers the unique opportunity to gain exposure to gold while also being able to make a profit and even improve cash flow via dividend stocks.

While this is an excellent investment option it shouldn't be considered an alternative to investing in physical gold. Stocks are driven by the price of gold but there are also other factors involved including the fundamentals of the mines, the reserves of unmined gold, projects and so on. Of course, it is these factors that offer investors the opportunity for capital appreciation.

However, as with any investment in equity, one needs to make sure to do their due diligence, which includes getting to know the mining industry, studying the financials of the company being considered and conducting technical analysis on both the price of gold as well as the stocks in question.

Gold Certificates

Gold certificates are simply ownership papers of physical gold, proving you own it even though it is being stored by the bank that issued the certificate. The advantages include the fact that you don't have to worry about insurance costs and storage as well as safety. Likewise, it's much easier to sell your gold this way because it can be done either online or via a phone call to the bank. Not all countries issue these gold certificates but they are more prevalent in Germany and Switzerland.
The Perth Mint also issues such certificates and they are backed by the government of Western Australia. It might be an option for you as they are distributed to quite a few other countries.

Gold Oriented Funds

These funds include a number of vehicles focused on collective investments, including mutual funds and unit trusts.

Some of these funds specialize in gold and equity in gold mining companies. You have to analyze each fund individually because they have different structures and objectives. Some will invest in shares looking for capital gains specifically in gold mining companies while others prefer value investments and look for companies that mine other minerals as well. Other differences include the types of assets the fund will invest in, with some preferring a more diverse approach, investing in futures as well as equity, while others might prefer a mix of physical gold and futures.

The type of fund you invest in is wholly determined by your goals and how you want your investment portfolio to be allocated. Remember, though, it is always a good idea to have some form of ownership of physical gold, especially if you are looking to hedge against currency devaluation.

The risk of investing in gold funds is the same as the risk of investing directly in the different financial instruments. The advantage, though, is that you can get exposure to a wider range of instruments than you could if you were to invest directly due to the collective nature of these funds.

Gold Structured Products

While structured products have a high entry barrier since they are designed mainly for large financial institutions, it is still worth taking a look at these products for a complete understanding of the gold market.

Forwards

Forwards are similar to futures except that they trade over the counter and usually the two parties involved will negotiate the price and date directly. Unlike futures, which are guaranteed by the exchange, forwards carry the risk of one of the parties not fulfilling the agreement. Another disadvantage to forward contracts is that the obligation cannot be transferred meaning the holding institution cannot sell it to another party before the contract matures.

Gold Backed Bonds and Structured Notes

Investors use gold backed bonds as a way to gain exposure to the fluctuations of gold price, to obtain a yield and for capital preservation. These bonds are issued by large investment banks and bullion dealers.

A structured note takes part of amount being invested and puts it into options while the rest goes towards more traditional products to try and generate capital gains.

Silver Investment Vehicles

Silver investment vehicles are, in most cases, exactly the same as gold. Thus, you can invest in silver via:

- Silver bars with a purity of 99.9%;
- Silver coins minted by governments;
- Medallions: pieces of round silver that look like coins but are not considered to be legal tender;
- Certificates or Storage Accounts;
- Accumulation plans;
- Futures contracts;
- Options;
- Exchange Traded Funds;
- Equity in mining specialized mining companies;
- Mutual Funds

Each of these comes with its own set of advantages and disadvantages. For example, if you opt for physical silver, such as bars, coins or medallions, you have a wide range of options because they tend to be the least expensive option and can be converted into cash anywhere in the world.

It is worth noting that no matter which investment vehicle you choose, the price of silver is much more volatile than gold. For example, at the beginning of 2011 it was trading at around $25 - $30, only to rise to almost $50 and fall back down towards the end of the year to around $29.

Thus, it is wise to take a more cautious approach when investing in silver. However, this volatility lends itself relatively well to making short-term profits, but as with any form of trading, there is also great risk of loss involved.

Beginners Basic Guide
to Investing in Gold and Silver Boxed Set

Chart courtesy of Kitco at www.kitco.com

Investing in Precious Metals

Now that we've looked at why you should invest in precious metals and what vehicles are available for you to do this, let's look at what you should be looking for when investing in precious metals.

Understand What You Are Investing In

First of all, no matter what type of investment vehicle you are opting for, you need to know the industry and sovereign fundamentals.

Industry fundamentals means that you have to analyze the gold and silver industry, including supply and demand, market sentiment and so on and so forth. However, as we revealed earlier, the state of the global economy can have a significant impact on the price of precious metals, which is why you should be looking at sovereign fundamentals as well.

Sovereign fundamentals have more to do with precious metals and currency. Basically, you are analyzing the financial statements of the major economies in the world, as we explained previously. The higher the chances of further quantitative easing being required, for example, the better the chance of the price of gold and silver going up as investors turn to these precious metals as a hedge.

The idea is that the better your understanding of the movements in price of gold and silver, the easier it will be for you to make the right call, especially since all investment vehicles for these precious metals are driven, at least in part, by the price of the underlying asset.

Besides fundamentals, you also need to look at the technical data of the gold, silver and currencies. This is because fundamental data will signal the existence or lack of an opportunity but technical data provides you with the timing. Technical analysis will allow you to pick the right moment to enter the market to ensure you get the maximum benefit from your investment. This applies no matter what your objective is because even if you simply want to purchase gold, for example, as a hedge, if the price is too high, you won't be able to hedge anything. So, timing is critical.

Make a Plan

You need to build an investment plan, no matter what type of investment you are making. However, with the numerous options available when it comes to precious metals, this is even more important. You need to decide what types of investment vehicles you will be using to gain exposure to precious metals and these depend mainly on your objectives.

For example, if your main goal is to purchase gold and silver as a hedge, then you will probably want to look towards purchasing the physical metal, either directly and taking delivery or via an ETF or Gold Pool Account.

Beginners Basic Guide to Investing in Gold and Silver Boxed Set

If your objective is capital appreciation, then you might consider purchasing equity in gold mining companies.

If you want to improve your cash flow, then you might opt to trade these metals on the markets, or look towards futures and options.

Then again, you can decide you want to do all three and use a mix of these vehicles, allocating various percentages of your available capital to each objective. The more risk averse you are, the more you should lean towards lower risk options, namely physical gold and silver, with a smaller portion of your investment portfolio being allocated to equity and other vehicles that provide capital gains.

Remember, any form of trading, namely buying and selling any of the investment vehicles we mentioned for short-term profit, carries substantial risk of losses so make sure to never invest money you cannot afford to lose.

Some questions the World Gold Council recommends you should answer before taking the leap include:

Why have you decided to purchase precious metals? What's your objective?

Do you want an asset that you can physically touch or gain access to at all times or do you simply want to take advantage of the price fluctuations of precious metals?

Do you want the precious metal delivered to your door or would you prefer the security of a vault?

Do you know exactly how much the transaction will cost, including all the taxes, commissions, premiums, storage and insurance?

Is the seller (either a dealer, broker or person) who you intend to buy from trustworthy and reliable?

What role will precious metals play in your investment portfolio and how will it fit in with the other investments you have?

These are just a few of the questions you need to answer before investing in precious metals.

Investing in Gold Equities

Investing in equities is quite different to investing in the physical asset itself since there are many more risks involved. However, there is also a better chance of capital appreciation so it's definitely worth taking a look at. We'll be looking mainly at investing in stocks in gold mining companies but the principles also apply to silver mining companies.

When it comes to investing in a gold mining company, the core principles of stock investing are the same. Thus, you should never put more money in the market than you can afford to lose. Just because a gold mining company is selling cheap, don't jump on the opportunity without doing your homework first because it could be a junior company who is only prospecting for gold. Since only one company in over two hundred finds gold, you could be looking at some completely worthless stock.

Therefore, it is critical that you do your homework first and ask who the promoter of the stock is. How effective has he or she been at creating wealth for investors? And you need to find out who the best performers in the industry are. And remember: never invest money you can't afford to lose.

As with the industry, you need to know exactly what you are buying. Dig up all the information you can on the company. Read their annual reports and not just the latest ones but go back a few years to see how the company performed both during good and bad times for the industry.

Remember that an economic boom generally means bad times for the gold industry so make sure to go back a few years and see how the company performed. Not only that, you might want to look at the management of the company as

Beginners Basic Guide
to Investing in Gold and Silver Boxed Set

well. All you have to do is call up and ask and you'll be surprised how willing these companies are to give you everything you need.

Often, small company stocks are sold by promoters. These are generally those phone calls or emails you get telling you about this amazing new stock in an up-and-coming super amazing gold company that you'll regret not buying into because stock prices will explode. Yes, you've probably had plenty of those.

However, not all of them are bad, but again, you need to do your due diligence. Investigate the person promoting the stock and see if they've ever had any problems, including fraud charges, tax evasions, bankruptcy proceedings and so on and so forth. You are looking for someone honest and if they've been in the business for a while and haven't had any issues, then they just might be for real. Remember that you can always ask your peers about their success with a particular promoter and that's an excellent way of finding out who is really good at what they do and not just at selling and promoting.

Greed is a killer in any form of financial investment or trading. It's what makes us hang on to those stocks when we know we should get out and take our profits and then we watch in horror as the market reverses and the shares drop in value. So, if you are investing in a junior company or looking for capital appreciation, don't wait an eternity to offload those stocks or you might find yourself on the losing end of the stick. If you want to invest in stocks that can keep you without worrying about volatility, consider dividend stocks as these will bring you a good annual return and the companies tend to be much more stable.

On the opposite end of the spectrum is fear of loss. People are generally terrified of losing even a penny, which can lead to investors keeping stocks that are clearly losers because they are hoping that by some miracle the market will reverse and they will at least break even. This is the best way to lose all your capital. Set a maximum amount you are willing to lose and once you hit that ceiling, get out. You might miss one or two profitable investments when the stocks retrace but that's a lot better than ending up with a pile of stocks that are worthless.

The Fundamentals of Gold Stocks or How to Improve Your Odds

There are so many small gold companies that it can be difficult to sort through them if you don't know exactly what fundamentals you should be looking at. The following fundamentals can be used to analyze any gold company, from the junior ones to the intermediate and senior gold companies.

Management

One factor few investors consider when analyzing a company is the management. You need to learn as much as you can about them and especially how much they know about the industry and what their training is. For example, are they geologists or lawyers? How much experience do they have in the industry? Do they really know what they are doing? The more effective the management team is, the better the chances of the company being successful over the long term, which implies better returns for the investor.

Market Capitalization

Market capitalization refers to the number of outstanding shares multiplied by the value of each individual share.

In other words, if a company has 3 million outstanding shares at $2 a piece, then the company is worth $6 million. The question you need to ask yourself is whether or not that company is worth $6 million.

One way to do that is to find out how many ounces of gold the company has in reserve, i.e. in the ground, and what the market price per ounce is. So, let's say they have half a million ounces in the ground and the market price is $100 per ounce, then the company should be valued at $50 million, which means the company is undervalued.

On the other end of the spectrum, if the company only has cash but no gold reserves, most investment strategists recommend that you shouldn't pay more than double the cash per share.

The key is to buy into companies that are undervalued because it provides a wider buffer of safety.

Money

If you are looking at a gold exploration company, you have to think like an entrepreneur. You need to remember that it takes time for any startup to start producing money and in mining it takes even longer with practically no cash flow coming in. These companies spend exorbitant amounts of money before they can sell their first ounce of gold.

As an investor, you need to determine what the chances of these delays taking place are and whether or not the company will have to find additional financing, usually through the sale of more shares. This is an even bigger problem if the company has been unable to make a find as it will lead to drastic drop in share price.

Minerals

When it comes to gold mining companies, those whose principal production is gold are valued higher than those that produce both gold and copper. However, when gold prices start to soar, these companies are treated exactly the same as those that produce only gold, which makes them a much better option for investors because they are cheaper to buy into.

Life of the Mine

When it comes to mining company stocks, these tend to be volatile, especially in the period before production begins. At first, when a find is made, stocks soar because every one is ecstatic thinking they are going to make a killing. However, when people realize it will take a while to actually get the gold out of the ground, prices drop. Additionally, there's the issue that some gold deposits simply can't be mined or are much too expensive to extract.

While the company is building the mine, the price of shares will remain stable and will only start to rise once the date of effective production gets closer. Once the mine is up and running, other factors intervene in the price of shares, including the management's ability to increase production, reserves and cash flow.

The more you know about what stage of the life cycle the company is in, the better your chances are of minimizing risk and increasing your returns.

A Few Closing Words about Investing in Precious Metals

Undoubtedly, investing in precious metals is a wise course of action but before you do, you need to ensure you have a good grasp of the industry and the market as a whole to minimize risk.

You need to establish your objectives, namely why you want to invest in precious metals, and you can then design your investment plan accordingly.

Economic Crisis: Surviving Global Currency Collapse - Safeguard Your Financial Future with Silver and Gold

Global Currency Collapse

In the event of global currency collapse, if there is no other currency available to take on the role of money, then it is likely the world will fall back on bartering to obtain the goods they need. In such a situation, it's hard to talk about capital preservation, as most people will be more interested in finding a way to feed their families and make sure they have shelter.

It might sound completely ludicrous but a currency collapse on a global level would lead to more than civil and social unrest. Once things settled down, it would still likely take a long time for people to learn to trust fiat currency again, which is why bartering will become the name of the game.

You have food and your neighbour has gas so you barter, agreeing on what would be considered a fair price. It is likely that gold and silver will start being used more and more often, as they have intrinsic value and have been used as money throughout the ages. So, it wouldn't be long before gold and silver become the standard currency, which is why it is so important that everyone safeguards their future by converting as many of their assets as possible into gold and silver.

Of course, this isn't to say you should convert your entire portfolio into precious metals. The risk of global currency collapse is present but there is no guarantee it will happen. And while investing in gold and silver is a good idea and certainly not a losing trade, it's also an investment likely to make substantial gains. Many investors choose to keep approximately one third of their portfolio in higher-risk and higher-gain investment with the remaining two thirds allocated to medium and low risk investments.

If you are risk adverse, your percentages might differ somewhat. However, the key is that you should be allocating a hefty portion of your portfolio to gold and silver. And regardless of the type of investment, it's probably a wise idea to buy physical gold and silver. Irrespective of what happens, whether it's worldwide currency collapse or all-out war, if you own physical gold and silver, it can always be traded for things you need.

Once currency collapses, the majority of your paper investments, including stocks, futures, options and so on and so forth, become virtually useless. This is why you need to make sure that you have plenty of gold in your portfolio and not just ETFs or mining stocks.

The Gold Standard vs Fiat Paper Currency

Gold coins have been used as money for thousands of years but there were problems with using gold as currency. This was because for normal trade, gold coins were too valuable to be used. In fact, they were mainly used by the wealthy for certain types of transactions, including paying taxes and business.

Eventually, as a solution so people didn't carry around vast amounts of wealth on them, paper currency was invented. Remember that prices were very different and one gold coin could buy you a few acres of land, so you can imagine how dangerous it could be carrying around so much wealth.

Paper money gradually came about, though there were various different other forms of currency used in lieu of gold, such as sticks with notches representing certain amounts of gold. Regardless of the type of currency, the common thing they all had was they were all based on gold. This eventually became known as the gold standard.

Historically speaking, the gold standard worked for a very long time and during that period, you could theoretically exchange a paper banknote for gold and the bank was obligated to give you the equivalent in gold. However, it was rarely practiced.

The way it worked was that people would deposit their gold coins in the bank's vault and receive paper currency in exchange. This paper money caught on quite quickly because it was easier to carry around, so it was definitely a lot more practical, and it was easier to break up the value of a coin into multiple notes, making it easier to trade.

Slowly, over the years, the gold standard evolved into the concept we know today, whereby a country couldn't issue more paper currency than the amount of gold in its reserves. It also meant that exchange rates were stable because many countries' currencies were valued against the price of gold.

However, there were problems with this because the price of gold tended to fluctuate just as it does now. In other words, if there was panic in the market or production was lower than expected, prices of gold would soar, which would lead to inflation. Conversely, when prices of gold would drop due to new gold veins being discovered, increased production or a booming economy, the market would suffer from deflation.

While the gold standard may not have been perfect, it did stop governments and central banks from manipulating the value of currency as they saw fit. The moment the gold standard was abolished, governments and central banks had the power to print money as they saw fit. They were no longer bound by any rules and regulations.

The problem with being able to issue money whenever one chooses is that the value of fiat currency is determined by a few factors, including supply and demand as well as the population's faith in that currency. Thus, the more fiat money is printed, the lower the value of one unit, in other words the fewer goods you can purchase for one unit of currency. An excess of currency can lead to hyperinflation and even a complete collapse of the value of paper money.

Fiat currency refers to any form of paper money that isn't tied to gold and its value is derived from the fact that the population accepts it as money and has faith in the government, which accepts payment in this form.

Now, the question arises regarding which option is better. Would the gold standard be preferable to the current fiat currency system? Many say no, because the price of gold cannot be controlled whereas the value of fiat currency can. This is true because a central bank can withdraw paper currency from the market and stabilize inflation or increase the supply to prevent deflation.

However, there is another problem that many don't realize. Many central banks are privately owned by large financial groups. And these financial groups aren't interested in ensuring people have a good lifestyle, which would mean balancing the supply of fiat currency to avoid inflation. They are interested in making money.

Take the Federal Reserve Bank as an example. The Fed is in charge of issuing currency. However, instead of just "handing" the money over to the government, they charge interest. Thus, practically, the government is forced to borrow money from its own central bank.

So, take the stimulus packages the US government used to attempt to restart the economy after the crash in 2008. Logically, you would think the best course of action would be to print more money to cover the debt, right? Well, that's not quite accurate.

Firstly, an increase in supply of paper currency leads to the devaluation of that currency. Secondly, since the government is practically borrowing from the Fed, it has to pay interest, which means an increase in the deficit. So, they'd have to print even more money to try and cover the deficit. However, the more they print, the more it will cost them and the less the dollar is worth. It's a vicious cycle that can lead to the complete collapse of paper currency.

Note that this is happening in much of Europe as well and in most western countries. Thus, it's not strictly relegated to the US.

So, does that mean the gold standard is a better option? It could be but just like the fiat currency system, it will only work if it's properly regulated. Remember, gold itself has value because people believe it does. It doesn't feed you or keep you warm. It's a piece of metal that's used in industrial applications and for jewelry mainly, so its real value comes from the fact that we believe it's valuable. Just like with paper currency.

So, either system can work effectively as long as there are proper rules and regulations in place. But this type of regulatory framework has to be established by a government that isn't being lobbied by private corporations every minute of the day and isn't worried about re-election but about sorting out the monetary system.

The main problem is that things will have to get a lot worse before they get better, because people have been used to living on debt for much too long, which is the main problem. You would think that the recent financial catastrophe would have taught us a lesson. It worked for about a year – maybe – but then people reverted to borrowing significant amounts and now, things are almost as bad in terms of individual debt levels as they were pre-crisis.

Central Banks and Bullion Gold

One thing is certain. When central banks start buying up gold, you have to wonder what's coming. These are the same people who, not long ago, claimed that gold was nothing more than a relic, a throwback to a different era and that those who sought it out as a hedge for their wealth were living in the past. They even sold off as much of their gold as they could, causing the price to plummet.

After such statements and actions, you wouldn't expect central banks to start buying up gold like it was going out of fashion. According to a report released by the World Gold Council on the 2011 gold market, overall investment in gold increased by a mere 5%. However, the volume of gold central banks bought increased by approximately 500% from 2010, a year which also showed a significant increase in central banks' appetite for gold.

So, what does this all mean? After all, they sold off all their gold, causing the price of gold to tank because of the massive supply that was suddenly available. And now they are buying it up at five or six times the price.

These are the people who convinced governments to abandon the gold standard to switch to fiat currencies, which they could only obtain from central banks at a cost. In other words, every unit of money printed brought debt along with it.

And now? central banks find themselves in the situation in which they are printing money for governments that can't afford to pay their debts. In other words, paper currency is slowly but surely heading downhill and soon it won't be worth the paper it's printed on.

What's even worse is that by buying up all this gold, they are further devaluing paper currency due to the message they are sending. Why should people store their savings in dollars, euros, yen or any other paper currency, when banks are converting their fiat money into gold?

So, essentially, it's a vicious cycle because central banks are sending out the message that they don't have faith in their own creation. It probably won't be long before we see a complete collapse of global currencies. At least that's what we can conclude from the fact that central banks purchased 440 tons of gold in 2011 versus 77 tons in 2010.

Gold vs. Silver

So, why is everyone so set on gold and silver? Why do all traders and investors seem to throw their money at gold and silver the moment they sense something might be wrong with the market?

The answers are quite simple. Gold and silver are considered precious metals and have been favoured by investors for a very long time as they maintain their inherent value, regardless of the state of the economy. Silver and gold are prized and rare metals. In the history of time they each have held their trading value well.

Of course, gold has always been the more valuable of the two precious metals but that is due to some of its unique properties as well as the fact that it is quite a bit rarer than silver.

Gold and Silver to Safeguard Your Financial Future

Clearly, investing in silver and gold will help protect your assets in the event of a worldwide currency collapse. While many people claim this can't happen, there are just as many signs pointing to it as a serious possibility. If global currency collapse does occur, you will need to have some form of wealth protection in place that not only ensures you are protecting the value of your assets but can also be converted into everyday items you will need.

In a situation in which all currencies across the globe have crashed, other markets will follow, starting with the stock market. The only things that will have true value are commodities. However, you will need to have a way to trade them, which is why it is a good idea to have physical gold stored in an easily accessible place.

Note that keeping everything in the bank might seem like a good idea but if currencies do crash, it won't be a pretty sight. People will see their life savings vanish in an instant. They will realize the money in their wallets can't even buy them a loaf of bread and they are no longer able to feed their families. This will lead to social unrest. So, you are better off keeping your physical gold in a safe location known to yourself only to ensure easy access in order to purchase goods required for the survival of your family.

Of course, even if the decline is more gradual and doesn't necessarily lead to social unrest, people will still likely switch over to using gold and silver as money because they will have more faith in a metal that has always maintained its value compared to paper money.

Thus, it's wise to have a relatively good portion of your investment portfolio allotted to gold and silver. You also might consider varying the types of investments you make. For example, when you invest in gold, you aren't limited to physical gold. There are many other options, including futures, gold exchange traded funds and more.

The mix you choose depends on your appetite for risk and the main reason you are investing in gold or silver. If you are looking to simply preserve your capital, then you probably want a solution that doesn't involve too much risk and that would generally be to invest in physical gold or silver.

Factors Affecting the Price of Gold and Silver

There are many things that have an impact on the prices of gold and silver but the more you understand about these precious metals and what makes them tick, the better your chances are of making the right investment decisions.

So, first and foremost, we have market sentiment. This is what many traders and investors forget, especially when they sit and stare at charts all day long. The market is comprised of human beings making human decisions. These decisions are not always logical nor are they necessarily right but human emotion will always play a part in the markets. This is why market sentiment is so important.

For example, let's presume that the economy seems to be going all right. Everything seems positive and, in fact, it actually is. However, someone has a different agenda and they launch a rumour saying a big bank is about to go under. The rumour is generally enough for people to withdraw their life savings and convert them into gold and silver. The result is that it drives up the price of gold and silver.

Historically speaking, if you look at the price of gold, during the economic boom it was relatively low since no one wanted to buy into gold. It was seen as a waste of time because it couldn't provide capital appreciation and who needed capital preservations during a boom.

However, things changed and suddenly, gold and silver became the most important investments possible because people couldn't believe what they were seeing. These companies and banks were too big to fail, weren't they? Unfortunately, no, they weren't. And as a result people turned to gold right away to protect themselves from a very uncertain future. After all, who knew what could happen?

Sadly, we find ourselves in much the same situation. We know something is going to happen and we doubt it's a good thing. It could be the collapse of global currencies or it could be a serious recession, bigger than the last one. And this is why many people are turning to gold, going on the principle that it's better to be safe than to be sorry, which is quite accurate.

Another factor that influences the price of gold and silver is, obviously, currency. The weaker the dollar is, for example, the higher the value of gold, when it comes to silver, supply and demand has an important impact on price. However, with gold, things differ. Gold doesn't move so significantly in terms of supply and demand because of the various stockpiles. It is well known that banks can influence the price of gold by withholding or releasing their reserves. For this reason, the market doesn't take much notice of supply and demand levels.

The value of currency, however, plays a much bigger role. The lower the value of currency, the more people will turn to gold to hedge their investments against inflation and complete currency collapse.

Fiscal and interest rate policies also have an influence on the price of gold and silver. The lower the interest rate is, the more people will be interested in purchasing commodities such as precious metals. If the interest rate is high, on the other hand, people tend to shift towards less risky alternatives, such as treasury bills and deposits. Otherwise, it would be very difficult to make a profit.

During economic growth, central banks raised interest rates to make credit more expensive. This way, they kept inflation under control. Unfortunately, the high interest rates also made it that no one was interested in precious metals because their growth potential was practically non-existent.

In terms of fiscal policies, the more currency a government decides to print and release into the economy, the lower the value of one unit of that currency will be. Thus, the more currency is printed, the higher the price of gold as more and more people turn to it to protect their assets.

Another factor that dictates the price of precious metals is the extraction and production process. Gold mining is becoming increasingly expensive and the rise in production costs as well as currency devaluation has all had an impact on the price of gold. There is less and less gold being produced every year because there isn't much gold left in areas that are easy to get to. Any new gold that has been found over the past few years has been in areas that are extremely difficult to mine.

Bureaucracy can also be an issue because getting mining permits can take as long as a decade, which, of course, drives up the price of gold. Then there are the price increases of all the other resources needed to mine gold, which also affect the price of gold itself by making it more expensive to mine.

Precious Metals: A Hedge for the Big Boys

The price of gold has gone up significantly because more and more large organizations are turning to gold to hedge their assets. As a result of the financial meltdown, many banks and financial institutions came to the realization that they needed to expand their portfolios and preferably with something tangible, hence so many turned to commodities. Thus, most companies chose to invest in gold in such a way that they could have access to the physical product rather than investing in paper alone. The liquidity of physical gold can't really be matched and, in the worst scenario, it can be traded for goods and services, even if currencies collapse completely.

**Beginners Basic Guide
to Investing in Gold and Silver Boxed Set**

Gold and Silver Investment Vehicles

So, now that you have a good idea of why you should invest in gold and silver and what drives the price of these precious metals, it's time to look at how you can invest in them.

There are a number of ways you can invest in gold and silver. You can either own it physically by purchasing coins or bullion or you can limit yourself to exposure to price fluctuations by investing in mining stocks, ETF and other financial instruments. The choice is yours but if you are looking to safeguard your financial future against global currency collapse, the best option will likely be to turn to physical gold and silver as it is more likely to maintain its value and is more liquid. Thus, it is easier to trade for the goods you might need, whereas stocks will become practically worthless in such a situation.

Investment Gold and Silver Bullion Coins

One great thing about purchasing gold bullion coins is that you can gain exposure to physical gold without having to make massive investments. It also doesn't hurt that you can change over gradually, buying small amounts at a time, until you reach a level you are pleased with. Note, that quite a few countries do not charge Value Added Tax on gold bullion coins, which doesn't hurt at all.

When it comes to gold bullion coins, you have lots of options because there are lots of countries that issue gold bullion coins. When it comes to the global market value of these coins, it is usually calculated according to the amount of gold included in the coin and a premium. On the other hand, in the country where they are minted, these coins are usually valued at the face value stamped on them.

The premium on gold coins varies according to a number of factors but the size of the coin plays a significant role as well. The smaller the coin, the higher the production cost, which means the premium will be higher. Note that the premium also includes the dealer's commission.

The same applies to silver bullion coins except that they have one major advantage over gold, namely that they are cheaper though silver maintains its value just like gold. In fact, many retail investors prefer silver over gold because the entry barrier is much lower. For example, the average price of gold was $1,571.52 per ounce in 2011, while the average price of silver was $35.12, which was considered a record high.

So, as you can imagine, it's much easier to start stocking up on silver than gold yet one can enjoy a similar degree of capital preservation.

Let's look at some of the more popular gold and silver coins.

Australian Gold Nugget and Gold Lunar Bullion Coins:

The Australian Gold Nugget is a gold bullion coin minted by the Perth Mint. They are produced in denominations of 1/20 oz, 1/10 oz, ¼ oz, ½ oz, 1 oz, 2 oz, 10 oz and 1 kg. In other words, there's an

Australian Gold Nugget that contains 1 kg of pure, 24k gold.

These coins have legal tender status in Australia and, surprisingly, they get a design makeover every year. Due to the fact that only a limited number of these coins are produced every year, these coins tend to have a higher value than just that of the gold content they include. However, regardless of the design, the coins always feature a kangaroo. They are also referred to as Gold Kangaroos.

The Australian Lunar coins are similar to the Gold Kangaroo or Gold Nugget in terms of denominations and gold content. The only real difference lies in the images minted on the coins. Instead of using the popular kangaroo, these coins feature images of different animals from the Chinese calendar.

Australian Kangaroo and Kookaburra Silver Bullion Coins

Like its gold counterpart, the Australian Silver Kangaroo is a silver bullion coin minted by the Perth Mint and despite the fact that every year it is redesigned, it always feature a kangaroo.

This silver bullion coin weighs one troy ounce, in compliance with international standards, which is the equivalent of 31.1 grams. It has a purity of 99.9% and a face value of $1 Australian dollar. While the coin is considered legal tender, it's not meant to be circulated.

The Australian Silver Kookaburra is considered to be the most popular Australian silver bullion coins. This is mainly due to their design, since it changes constantly, featuring a different image on the reverse of the coin. While many other silver bullion coins are available in sizes of one troy ounce and fractional sizes such as ½ ounce coins, the Silver Kookaburra is only available as a 1 ounce, 2 ounce, 10 ounce and 1 kilogram coin.

Australian Lunar and Koala Silver Bullion Coins

The Australian Silver Lunar coin features images based on the progression of the Chinese zodiac, which makes it a highly desirable coin for collectors. Thus, every year a Silver Lunar coin is minted in accordance with the Chinese zodiac, featuring the respective animal. For example, 2011 was the Year of the Rabbit and a rabbit was featured on the coin.

The Australian Silver Koala is a relatively new silver bullion coin as it was first minted in 2007. It features a koala, as you would expect. It is available as a one ounce, 10 ounce and 1 kilogram coin.

Austrian Philharmonic Gold Bullion Coins

The Austrian Philharmonic is one of the most popular gold coins in Europe. In fact, in 2008 it was the most popular in the world, as the 1oz denomination sold more units than U.S. Eagles or Krugerrands. This coin is minted in one-ounce, half-ounce, quarter ounce and one tenth ounces.

Austrian Silver Vienna Philharmonic Coin

The Austrian Silver Vienna Philharmonic is a silver bullion coin that is practically identical in design with its gold counterpart. It was first minted in 2008 and has a purity of 99.9% silver. They are highly popular due to the exquisite design, being considered the most beautiful silver bullion coins in Europe.

Canadian Maple Leaf

The Canadian Maple Leaf was first minted in 1979 and represented Canada's entry into the competitive gold bullion market. It is minted in one-ounce, half an ounce, quarter of an ounce and one tenth ounce sizes. In 2008, due to the financial crisis, the sale of these coins increased dramatically as people struggled to protect their assets. Thus, instead of 278,600 ounces being sold, which was the number for 2007, in 2008 896,000 ounces were sold, making for more than triple the sales.

Canadian Silver Maple Leaf

The Canadian Silver Maple Leaf is a silver bullion coin that was first minted in 1988 by the Royal Canadian Mint. It features a 99.99% level of purity, marking it as the silver bullion coin with the highest degree of silver purity in the world. The coin usually has a maple leaf on it.

Chinese Panda Gold Bullion Coins

The Chinese Panda differs from other gold coins in two main ways. First of all, the Panda design on the back of the coin changes every year and, secondly, each coin is minted as a limited edition.

These coins are minted in 1 oz, ½ oz, ¼ oz and 1/10 oz and 1/20 oz denominations. This gold bullion coin was first introduced in 1982.

Chinese Panda Silver Bullion Coins

The Chinese Silver Panda was first minted in 1983 and every year it has featured a different panda design. This often makes it more expensive than other silver bullion coins due to higher premiums. This silver bullion coin contains 1 troy ounce of silver and has a purity of 99.9%.

South African Krugerrand Gold Bullion Coins

The South African Krugerrand was first minted in 1967. The idea was to help market and export gold from South Africa. The coin became quite popular and, surprisingly, by 1980 it represented 90% of the market in terms of gold coins in the world.

The South African Krugerrand actually served as the inspiration for many other countries to mint their own coins, including Canada, Australia, the U.S. and the U.K.

United Kingdom Britannia Gold Bullion Coins

The Britannia coins are British gold bullion coins issued by the Royal Mint. The gold coins date back to 1987. In 1997, a silver version went into production.

Gold Britannia coins are minted in one ounce, half ounce, quarter ounce and tenth ounce denominations.

United Kingdom Silver Bullion Coins

Silver Britannia coins are a highly popular silver bullion coin but only feature a 95.84% degree of silver purity, which is surprising as it makes it the least pure coin on the market. However, it should be noted that each coin still contains one troy ounce of silver, except that the actual weight of the coin is higher due to the lower purity. It has a face value of £2 but its current market value exceeds £30.

USA - Buffalo and American Eagle

The American Gold Eagle is the official gold bullion coin of the United States and was first released in 1986. It is authorized under the Gold Bullion Coin Act of 1985 and is available in 1/10 oz, ¼ oz, ½ oz and 1 oz denominations. The gold purity of the coins is 22 karat and, by law, the gold used in these coins must come from America.

There are also silver and platinum versions of this coin.

The American Buffalo was first minted in 2006 and is the first time a pure gold bullion coin of 24k was minted by the United States government.

USA - American Silver Eagle

The American Silver Eagle was first minted in 1986 and is considered the official silver bullion coin of the United States. It is available as a one-ounce coin with a 99.9% degree of silver purity.

Regardless of the type of coin you choose to purchase, remember that you will pay a larger premium for smaller coins. Additionally, consider that it might be a better idea to purchase bars since they come with a smaller premium. The production system isn't quite as complicated as it is with coins.

Gold and Silver Bars

Gold bars are another excellent way one can invest in physical gold. In fact, sometimes they are the better option because they don't carry such a high premium compared to coins. Another advantage is that there are so many different bars available in terms of size that the choice is practically limitless. This makes it easy for anyone to invest in gold.

Note that the purity of the gold content in bars is generally around 99.5% but it can differ. Gold bars are used significantly in the jewelry and industrial sectors but are often preferred by investors because of the low entry barrier. The smaller the gold bar, the cheaper it is to purchase.

In terms of silver, many prefer silver bullion bars since they are easy to store due to their rectangular shape. Like gold, they are available in a wide range of sizes, starting at 1 oz bar going all the way up to 1,000 oz bars, which weigh about 31 kg. Note that silver bars have a purity of 99.9%.

A highly popular silver bar for investment is the 100 oz bar, which weighs 3.11 kg. Its popularity stems from the fact that it features a lower premium than one would have to pay for purchasing 100 bars weighing one ounce or 10 bars weighing ten ounces. This bar makes sense for the retail investor because one can save money on premiums while still making a reasonable investment.

Storing Silver and Gold

Once you've started investing in silver and gold bullion, you'll face a logistical issue, namely where and how to store your investment. There are a few options and each carries its own advantages and disadvantages. Thus, you can store the bullion yourself or allow a third party to hold it for you.

Storing the Bullion Yourself

If you don't have a large quantity of bullion, whether it's silver or gold, you have the option of storing it at home. Of course, you will have to find a secure place for it, like a safe or some other concealed location.

Some people think burying their bullion is a good way to protect it from being stolen, as many did during the Great Depression, but this isn't exactly the best course of action. First of all, when it comes to silver, it is highly corrosive and it should be handled as little as possible. Burying it in the ground will only devalue the silver content. The longer it stays in the ground, the more money you lose.

Let's not forget that many people have buried their precious metals only to forget where they buried them. This was a common problem for people during the Great Depression as they buried cash and bullion to keep it from being confiscated by the government only to forget where it was buried. Then, some lucky homeowner who purchased the property years later made a stunning discovery.

While storing your bullion at home is not the most advisable course of action, if you do decide to go down this route, you should take some precautions. Firstly, don't store all your fortune in one place. If you do get robbed, at least you have a chance of saving some of your bullion this way.

Of course, you want to ensure you conceal it as well as possible but you also have to remember where you hid it. Additionally, make sure you don't tell anyone about the bullion in your home, including your friends. You never know what they might let slip and to whom, which could make you target of thieves.

Storing Your Bullion in a Safety Deposit Box

A better option is to store your bullion in a safety deposit box at a reputable bank. However, it is imperative that you only store your gold or silver with a bank that is financially sound because if they do become insolvent, you risk being unable to access your safety deposit box because you simply wouldn't be able to get into the bank.

There are also other drawbacks, including the potential failure of the world banking system or even the government deciding to confiscate physical gold, which would not be a first. Note, though, that there are some countries where this is less likely to happen so if you have a large amount of gold, you might want to opt for a safety deposit box overseas.

When deciding which bank to store your bullion in, you need to take a good look at the bank's results. If it has a history of weathering financial storms well, then it's a good bet your bullion will be safe.

Storing Your Investment with a Bullion Dealer

Many bullion dealers not only sell silver and gold bullion but also provide storage services in exchange for a fee. This is often a good choice because it is safer than storing it at home and it's also easier to turn your gold or silver into cash if necessary. Additionally, there is less risk because there is no transportation required.

Note that some bullion companies will offer insurance within the fee while with others, you will have to take out a policy yourself.

Diversification

The best way to store your bullion would be to diversify, just like you would with your investment portfolio. It's a good idea to have a little bullion in your home in the event of an emergency. However, you probably should consider storing the majority within secure vaults, like those offered by banks either through safety deposit boxes or allocated storage, or commercial bullion companies.

In fact, it might be an idea to split your investment up between the three types to minimize your risks. If you have your gold and silver spread out over three or more vaults, if one bank or company becomes insolvent, you will still be able to easily access the remainder of your bullion.

But it's imperative that you do your research to make sure you are handing your bullion over to a company or financial institution that has a good reputation and is financially sound.

Conclusion

In the event of global currency collapse, gold and silver are the only things you will be able to count on to maintain their value. While you might think that complete devaluation of world currencies is impossible, remember that nothing is impossible. You could wake up one morning to see that the dollar has crashed and isn't even worth the paper it's printed on.

For this reason, everyone should be prepared. One can't know how people will react when they discover their life savings have been erased and the money they have in their wallets isn't worth anything. That's why it's best to have something of value to trade and nothing is more valuable than gold or silver.

And by converting part of your savings into gold right now, you won't need to worry about being among those who will lose all their savings when currencies collapse. If you have all your savings in a deposit account then the first thing you need to do is convert part of it into gold and silver. Buy bullion coins or gold certificates or buy into a gold allocated account. Regardless of what course of action you take, make sure you have access to physical gold because that's what will count. Stocks and other paper financial instruments will be useless but gold and silver bars or coins will rule.

Warning: Your capital is at risk when you invest in futures, stocks and commodities - you can lose some or all of your money, so never risk more than you can afford to lose. Always seek professional advice if you are unsure about the suitability of any investment. Past performance is not a reliable indicator of future results.

Beginners Basic Guide to Investing in Gold and Silver Boxed Set

Glossary of Gold and Silver Bullion Terms

Ask: the price at which a dealer offers to sell.

Assay: a test to ascertain the fineness and weight of a precious metal.

Bid: the price at which a dealer is willing to buy.

Boiler room: an enterprise that uses high pressure sales tactics, false or misleading information, and scare tactics, generally over the telephone, to sell overpriced or worthless investments to unsophisticated investors.

Bullion: precious metals in the form of bars that are at least 99.5% pure.

Bullion coin: a coin with a symbolic face value but trades at a price relative to its intrinsic value.

Call: the right, but not an obligation, to buy a commodity or a financial security on a specified date in the future.

Canadian Maple Leafs: modern bullion coins minted by the Royal Canadian Mint.

Chameleon: a broker or dealer who changes his position on an investment to what he thinks will cause an investor to enter into a transaction.

Comex: one of the world's major commodities futures exchanges where gold and silver are traded. The Comex is in New York City and is a division of the New York Mercantile Exchange.

Fiat money: paper money made legal tender by law, although not backed by gold or silver.

Gold standard: a monetary system based on convertibility into gold; paper money backed and interchangeable with gold.

Hallmark: mark or stamp on a bullion item that identifies the producer.

Intrinsic value: the value of a coin's metal content.

Kilo bar: a bar weighing one kilogram (32.1507 troy ounces).

Koala: Australian platinum coin, minted since 1987, .995 fine.

Krugerrand: South African gold coin.

Liquidity: the quality of being readily convertible into cash.

NYMEX: the New York Mercantile Exchange, a future exchange where platinum and palladium are traded.

PCGS: acronym for Professional Coin Grading Service, one of two major coin grading services in the United States.

Silver Eagles: modern 1-oz silver bullion coins.

Uncirculated: a coin in new condition, sometimes said to be "brilliant uncirculated" or "BU." The term is often used interchangeably with Mint State.

Beginners Basic Guide
to Investing in Gold and Silver Boxed Set

Suppliers of Investment Quality Gold and Silver Bullion Bars and Coins

ATS BULLION LTD
International Bullion Merchants

http://www.atsbullion.com

Weighton Coin Wonders

Specialists in Gold and Silver Coins & Sets

http://www.weightoncoin.co.uk

Tax Free Gold Coins & Bars
www.taxfreegold.co.uk

American Precious Metals Exchange

APMEX is one of the largest and most active precious metal dealers.

http://www.apmex.com

Beginners Basic Guide to Investing in Gold and Silver Boxed Set

Chards is a leading UK coin and bullion dealer.
http://www.chards.co.uk

Gold and Silver Bullion Bars and Coins
Delivery is offered to all residents in the UK and within the EU
http://www.bullionuk.com

The Perth Mint Australia
Perth Mint, Western Australia, manufactures and distributes platinum, silver and gold coins.
http://www.perthmint.com.au

If you would like to share this book with another person, please purchase an additional copy for each recipient. Thank you for respecting the hard work of this author.